Pocket Explorer

The
Roman Empire

Sam Moorhead

INTERLINK BOOKS
An imprint of Interlink
Publishing Group, Inc.
www.interlinkbooks.com

Author's Acknowledgements
I would like to thank those colleagues who have provided images and comments on the text: Richard Woff, Richard Abdy, Eleanor Grey, Paul Roberts, Ralph Jackson, Ivor Kerslake, Jonathan Tubb, Don Bailey, John Williams, Roger Tomlin, David Stuttard, Gregory Powell and Anya Pakhamoff. Especial thanks are due to Carolyn Jones and David Sutherland who have worked with much patience on this project.

First American edition published 2011 by
INTERLINK BOOKS
An imprint of Interlink Publishing Group, Inc.
46 Crosby Street, Northampton, Massachusetts 01060
www.interlinkbooks.com

Text copyright © Sam Moorhead, 2008 & 2010

Library of Congress Cataloging-in-Publication Data available.
ISBN: 978-1-56656-828-9

Designed by Crayon Design, Brighton
Printed in Singapore by Tien Wah Press

To request our complete 40-page full-color catalog, please call us toll free at 1-800-238-LINK or visit our website at www.interlinkbooks.com

Illustration Acknowledgements
Main map artwork by Cally Sutherland, Crayon Design, Brighton.
Photographs are of objects in the British Museum, copyright the Trustees of the British Museum, unless otherwise noted below.

Richard Abdy 8 bottom, 9 centre right, 9 bottom right, 13 centre right, 17 centre left, 17 bottom left,
© Georg Gerster/Panos Pictures 7 top left, 10 top, 24 top.
Eleanor Grey 18 bottom left.
Ralph Jackson 15 centre right, 15 top right.
Ivor Kerslake 19 top left.
Sam Moorhead 4 right, 6 bottom, 7 top centre, 13 bottom left, 14 top right, 16 centre left, 16 bottom left, 17 top left, 18 top right, 19 bottom right, 20 left, 20 bottom right, 21 top left, 21 top right, 23 centre bottom, 24 bottom left, 25 bottom right, 26 bottom right, 27 centre, 28 bottom right, 29 top left, 30 right, 31 centre right.
© NTPL/Ian Shaw 29 centre right.
Anya Pakhamoff 13 centre left.
© Craig Perhouse/Lonely Planet Images 8 top.
Paul Roberts 7 bottom, 12 bottom right, 31 top right.
David Sutherland 3.
Roger Tomlin (drawing) 29 top right.
Jonathan Tubb 23 bottom right.
John Williams (© Trustees of the British Museum) 25 top right, 27 bottom right.

Contents

Birth and Running of Empire

Forget not, Roman, that it is your special genius to rule the peoples; to impose the ways of peace, to spare the defeated, and to crush those proud men who will not submit.

(Virgil, *Aeneid*)

Legend tells us that Rome was founded by Romulus in 753 BC. The early town grew from villages spread over the Seven Hills of Rome. Rome was ruled by Etruscan kings from 625 BC, but in 507 BC the Romans threw out these overlords and founded the Roman Republic. At the heart of government was the Senate of about three hundred aristocrats. The people elected magistrates every year from the senators, such as the two consuls who were the senior judges, and generals.

The Senate House in Rome, rebuilt after a fire in around AD 300.

The Republic began to conquer lands around the Mediterranean, or 'Our Sea' as the Romans called it. The expansion of this new empire led to the rise of highly ambitious men such as Pompey the Great, Crassus and Mark Antony. Two even assumed the emergency office of 'dictator', meaning sole ruler. This was supposed to be a temporary measure, but Julius Caesar assumed the title of 'Dictator For Ever'. He was assassinated on the Ides of March, 44 BC, by Romans who thought one man alone should not rule Rome.

However, Caesar had paved the way for a single ruler. Seventeen years later, in 27 BC, Octavian assumed the title of 'Augustus'

Statuette of a *lictor*, an official who helped the magistrates in the administration of government and law.

('Exalted') and became the first emperor of Rome. Augustus was popular because he brought peace and prosperity to the Roman world after years of civil wars. He was also a clever politician. Although he held ultimate power, he did preserve elements of the Republican government such as the Senate.

Silver coin of Julius Caesar, titling him 'Dictator Forever'.

Augustus united the empire, which had almost fifty provinces run by governors. Governors, who were normally senators, were responsible for the army, law and order in their provinces.

Procurators managed the provincial finances, collecting taxes and paying Roman soldiers and state officials. Any Roman on official

Gold coin of Augustus.

business could travel across the empire using the imperial postal service, which provided fresh horses and inns for overnight stays.

Tomb of Julius Classicianus, procurator in Britain in the AD 60s.

📜 Imperial documents

In the Mediterranean world papyrus, made from the Egyptian papyrus plant, was used for official documents. In the more northerly provinces people used wooden tablets, such as those found at Vindolanda on Hadrian's Wall in Britain. In the western half of the empire, people mainly wrote and spoke Latin; in the eastern half it was more often Greek.

Vindolanda tablet, which records the activities of soldiers in the First Cohort of Tungrians.

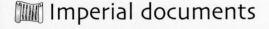

5

Italia and Sicilia: Heart of Empire

Sicily was the first to teach our ancestors what a fine thing it is to rule over foreign nations

(Cicero, *Verrine Orations*)

Roman money bar of the third century BC showing an elephant.

Between 496 BC and 290 BC, the Romans gradually conquered the peoples of Italy: the Etruscans, Latins, Sabines and Samnites. However, in 280–75 BC Rome was invaded by King Pyrrhus of Epirus, from Greece. His army included the first elephants the Romans had ever seen. Pyrrhus won several battles, but he lost vast numbers of his men and could not conquer Rome. This gave rise to the expression a 'Pyrrhic victory', meaning a victory won at too great a cost.

Carthage, in North Africa, was an even greater threat to Rome. Carthage had an empire which included Spain. Between 264 and 146 BC, Rome fought and won three wars against the Carthaginians. The Romans suffered some terrible defeats at the hands of the Carthaginian general Hannibal, notably the battle of Cannae in 216 BC where 50,000 Romans died. When Carthage was finally crushed, the Romans totally destroyed the city and ploughed salt into the soil to stop crops growing again.

Houses at Carthage with later, Roman, piers in the background.

After the defeat of Hannibal in 202 BC, Italy was able to rebuild. Many towns grew in size and new towns were founded. Lots of building took place during the reign of the emperor Augustus (31 BC–AD 14). Rome was adorned with many fine buildings such as forums (market-places), the Colosseum, the imperial palace on the Palatine Hill, the Basilica of Trajan, Hadrian's Pantheon and the Baths of Caracalla.

Rome also built new ports at Ostia and Portus at the mouth of the River Tiber. These harbours received the ships that brought food, wine, oil, stone, metals and other goods for the city.

Coin of Nero with a bird's eye view of Rome's port at Ostia.

Central Rome, showing the Colosseum, the Roman Forum and the Forums of Trajan and Augustus.

A street with stepping stones and cart-ruts in Pompeii.

In the Bay of Naples, the towns of Pompeii and Herculaneum flourished, before their destruction by the eruption of Mount Vesuvius in AD 79. The excavation of these towns has given us amazing insights into the everyday life of Roman towns in Italy.

Sicilia, first province of empire

The island of Sicily became the first province of Rome in 241 BC, after the first war with Carthage. It became an important source of horses and grain for Rome. Cato wrote that Sicily was 'the Republic's granary, the nurse at whose breast the Roman people is fed.' We know that the emperor Hadrian once climbed Sicily's Mount Etna to watch the sun rise. The governors of provinces were not always honest. Verres, a governor of Sicily, was prosecuted for corruption.

Roman amphitheatre, used for gladiator fights, at the Sicilian city of Syracuse.

7

Greece: Culture for Rome

Greece captured the savage victor, and brought her art to rustic Latium [Rome]

(Horace, *Epistles*)

Greek language and culture from cities such as Athens had already spread across the Mediterranean world as Greek people travelled and traded. When the Greek general Alexander the Great (336–23 BC) conquered his vast empire, he took Greek culture with him. Rome conquered Greece in 167 BC, creating three provinces: Macedonia, Epirus and Achaea.

The Acropolis at Athens.

Many Romans respected Greek culture, but the ruthless Roman general Mummius still sacked the Greek city of Corinth in 146 BC, and shipped many statues and other Greek works of art back to Rome. Several Roman civil wars were fought on Greek soil.

Julius Caesar defeated Pompey at Pharsalus in central Greece in 48 BC. Octavian (later the emperor Augustus) defeated Antony and Cleopatra off the west coast of Greece at the Battle of Actium in 31 BC.

Greek learning and culture had an enormous influence on Rome. The Greeks became the most respected doctors in the Roman empire. The Greek Galen became doctor to the Roman emperor Marcus Aurelius. Marcus Aurelius himself was a follower of Greek stoic philosophy,

Tower of the Winds in the Roman Forum at Athens with the Acropolis in the background.

which taught that one should do one's duty without complaint. He wrote his famous *Meditations* in Greek, not Latin, and his words still survive to advise us today.

Many Romans studied philosophy and the art of public speaking at Athens and other Greek cities. Rome's greatest orator, Cicero, learnt his art in Rhodes and his many writings were heavily influenced by Greek learning. The Romans also adapted Greek art and architecture for their own buildings.

The 'philosopher emperor' Marcus Aurelius (AD 161–80).

The Roman theatre in Athens, built by Herodes Atticus.

Roman citizens liked to watch comic plays of the Greek author Menander, which were translated into Latin by Plautus. Traditional Greek games, such as the Olympics, remained popular under Roman rule and many athletes from across the empire earned large sums of money. The emperor Nero even won a singing event at the Olympics, an event celebrated on one of his coins.

Copper coin showing Nero playing the lyre.

Hadrian, the 'Little Greek'

Hadrian became emperor in AD 117. He loved Greek culture and preferred to speak Greek instead of Latin, so he was nicknamed Graeculus, 'Little Greek'. In Athens, he built a famous library, completed the massive temple of Zeus and dedicated a new arch. Hadrian was also initiated into the Greek mystery religion of Demeter at Eleusis, near Athens.

The Temple of Zeus in Athens, completed by Hadrian, was the largest temple in the Roman empire.

9

North Africa: Corn and Animals for Empire

West of Mount Atlas there are forests full of animals that Africa produces ...
there are many crocodiles and hippopotamuses   (Pliny the Elder, *Natural History*)

North Africa was one of the richest parts of the Roman empire, but its conquest involved some of Rome's bloodiest wars. In 146 BC, Rome defeated Carthage, the city of Hannibal, who had come close to taking Rome. Rome then gradually occupied Africa from Morocco to Egypt. Africa was split into several provinces: Mauretania, Numidia, Africa Proconsularis, Cyrenaica, and Egypt (see p. 26).

Remains of the city of Leptis Magna.

North Africa was a much more fertile region in Roman times than it is now. In modern times the Sahara Desert has spread much further north. In Roman times Africa had enormous estates that produced wheat, wine and olives in vast quantities. Julius Caesar demanded an annual tribute of three million pounds of oil from the city of Leptis Magna. The wheat was even more important.

It was shipped directly to Rome to feed the million or so occupants of the imperial city, many of whom received free bread daily. Other important African exports were fish sauces (*garum* and *liquamen*) which were produced on an industrial scale at places such as Lixus in the province of Mauretania.

Fish and fruit mosaic from Carthage.

From across the Sahara came gold from West Africa, but also the threat of Berber goats who could destroy the wheat fields of the Roman provinces. The emperor Hadrian (AD 117–38) built a wall along the desert edge, called the *Fossatum Africae*, to keep the nomadic tribesmen and their animals out of the Roman crops. However, the animals that really interested the Romans were wild beasts, such as lions, elephants, bears and crocodiles, which were 'hunted' in amphitheatres across the empire.

Animal hunt mosaic from Utica, near Carthage.

We know that hundreds of wild animals could be killed in a day in the Colosseum in Rome. There was a massive industry which caught and transported living animals to Rome and other major cities. The demand for animals was so large that it caused local extinctions of species.

Silver coin of Septimius Severus showing animals and chariots in the arena.

Famous Africans

North Africa was the home of many rich senatorial families and even some emperors, including Septimius Severus. He was born in Leptis Magna, defeating several rivals to gain the empire in AD 193. His city was much enlarged as a result. Many famous writers also lived in North Africa. The Christian Bishop of Hippo, St. Augustine, wrote a famous book *The City of God* after the fall of Rome to the Goths in AD 410. When Carthage fell only 29 years later, the Western Roman empire lost her most valuable province and this hastened the decline of the city of Rome.

Statue of Septimius Severus (AD 193–211).

Hispania: Metals for Empire

Spain has long been the major source of gold in the world, producing, it is said, 20,000 pounds a year

(Pliny the Elder, *Natural History*)

Spain and Portugal (called Hispania by the Romans) had formed a major part of the Carthaginian empire. Hannibal had even founded Carthago Nova (New Carthage) as the Carthaginian capital in Spain. In 206 BC, at the end of the second war between Rome and Carthage, the Roman general Scipio Africanus finally drove the Carthaginians from Spain. Over the next two hundred years, Rome gradually conquered the whole land until under Augustus all of Spain was taken. Many Spaniards were recruited into the Roman army, especially as cavalrymen, and they served all over the empire.

A diploma granting citizenship to Reburrus, a Spanish cavalryman who served with a Panonnian unit in Britain.

The Romans settled many veteran Roman soldiers in Spain. Julius Caesar and Augustus alone founded twenty-one colonies of veterans. Spain produced many famous soldiers, senators and emperors. The emperor Trajan (AD 98–117) came from the Spanish city of Italica, and so did his adoptive son Hadrian (AD 117–38). In addition, many famous writers came from Spain. The philosopher Seneca, who was an adviser to the emperor Nero, and the historian Lucan both came from Corduba.

Spanish olive oil amphora, now used as a grave-marker in the Protestant Cemetery in Rome.

Columella, a native of Cadiz, wrote a book on farming which was popular across the empire. This is appropriate as Spain and Portugal were rich agricultural regions and

Bust of Trajan.

attracted many Roman settlers and merchants. Spanish olive oil was especially famous. It was transported in large amphorae (pottery jars) as far away as Hadrian's Wall in northern Britain.

Under the emperors, Spain had a long period of peace and stability. Only one legion was needed to keep order in the province. As a result many Spanish cities grew in size with aqueducts, amphitheatres and theatres.

Gold coin of Hadrian showing the representation of Spain seated with a rabbit. Ancient authors wrote that rabbits were originally native to Spain.

Far left: The Roman aqueduct at Segovia.

Left: The longest-surviving Roman bridge in the Roman empire at Merida.

Metal mining in Spain

Hispania was famous for its mineral wealth. The Rio Tinto valley in southern Spain and the Asturian mountains in northern Spain produced enormous amounts of gold, silver, copper, tin, lead and iron. Gold and silver were made into coins to pay the army and state employees and to finance imperial projects like the building of temples, amphitheatres and baths. Copper and tin were used to make bronze. Iron was essential for weapons, tools and construction. Lead was made into coffins, bath-linings and piping.

Roman mining wheel from Rio Tinto.

Lead pipe used at the Roman baths in Bath.

13

Gaul: Wine and Pottery for Empire

The Gauls are exceedingly fond of wine   Diodorus Siculus, *World History*)

The province of Gaul included all of modern France and parts of Belgium and Germany. The southern parts of the region, nearest to the Mediterranean and the Alps (modern Provence), had been part of the Roman world since the second century BC. The cities of Marseilles and Narbonne became important ports because they stood on important trading routes to northern Gaul and even Britain. Wine, glass and crafted metal objects travelled north from the Mediterranean, whilst slaves, metals such as tin, timber and agricultural produce came south.

Mosaic at Ostia outside the office of the traders from Narbo.

In 58–52 BC Julius Caesar conquered the many tribes of northern and eastern Gaul (between Switzerland, Belgium and Brittany). His wars of conquest are legendary and his victory was finally secured with the crushing defeat of the Gallic king Vercingetorix at Alesia.

Roman silver coin showing a Gaulish chieftain, possibly Vercingetorix.

Gaul developed fast and became one of the richest provinces of the western Roman empire. Wine was a major product in the south and Gaulish wine amphorae (jars) have been found all around the Roman world. There were also large agricultural estates which supported luxurious villas. These landowners were able to afford rich silver dining sets, such as the one found at Chaource.

Wine amphorae, probably from France, found in a British aristocrat's grave at Welwyn City, around 30 BC.

Gaul became home to the largest number of Roman senators outside Italy. Rich Romans lived in the cities of southern Gaul and today we can still see magnificent Roman buildings at St. Rémy, Arles, Orange and Nîmes.

Roman temple at Nîmes, called the Maison Carreé.

In the north, the origins of cities like Paris date from the Roman period. At Lyons, there was an altar erected to Augustus and Rome, showing the emperor's divine status. The area of Brittany was an important source of silver, lead and tin.

A selection of silverware used for drinking and dining from the Chaource hoard.

Roman arch and cenotaph at St. Rémy (Glanum).

Coin of Augustus from Lyons showing the Altar of Roma and Augustus.

 # Samian pottery

One of the most common forms of pottery used in the Roman empire was red Samian ware. It is found from Syria to Scotland. This ware was originally made in Arezzo in Italy, but in the reign of Augustus its production moved to Gaul. Hundreds of potters, whose names are stamped on the vessels, set up business on an industrial scale. Samian ware can be dated quite precisely, so it is the archaeologist's best friend.

A Samian ware pot, decorated with a hunting dog, found in England.

The River Rhine:
Rome's German Frontier

Germany is fertile for crops but not fruit trees. The people take pride in the quantity of their cattle which are their only greatly prized wealth. Silver and gold have been denied them by the gods.

(Tacitus, *Germania*)

The river Rhine flows northwards from Switzerland and Germany into the North Sea. The emperor Augustus tried to expand his empire beyond the Rhine, but in AD 9 the Germans crushingly defeated three of his legions. Augustus withdrew his army and the Rhine became the frontier with Germany However, the Romans did gain some important victories over the next hundred years.

This sword scabbard shows the emperor Tiberius presenting a statuette of Victory to the seated emperor Augustus. The sword was probably made around AD 15 for a senior officer who had fought in the wars against the Germans.

The reconstructed gateway of the Roman fort at Saalburg.

Legionary fortresses were built at places such as Nijmegen in Holland and Xanten, Cologne and Mainz in Germany. Pliny the Elder, the famous Roman writer who told us about the eruption of Vesuvius in AD 79, was a cavalry commander in Germany. The emperors Domitian (AD 81–96) and Hadrian (AD 117–38) built some major frontier works (called *limes*) beyond the Rhine. These were held by Rome until around AD 260 when the Rhine once again became the frontier.

A coin showing the emperor Domitian standing over a human representation of the River Rhine.

A reconstruction of the Roman frontier *limes*, near Saalburg.

The Rhine kept out invaders until the fifth century AD, when many different barbarian tribes finally crossed. The largest invasion came on 31 December 406, when the Vandals and others crossed the frozen Rhine.

A silvered-bronze disc from a horse harness, inscribed with the name of the Roman writer Pliny the Elder (AD 23-79), found at the fortress of Xanten.

The Imperial Baths in the Roman city of Trier.

The Audience Hall in the Palace at Trier.

The local population quickly took on Roman ways and many became Roman soldiers and citizens. Roman auxiliary troops recruited from the Tungrians and Batavians in northern Germany served in Britain at Vindolanda on Hadrian's Wall. Julius Classicianus, the procurator sent to Britain after the Boudican Revolt of AD 60–61, came from the Treveri tribe whose main centre was the city of Trier on the River Moselle. Trier became one of the capitals of the Roman empire in the third and fourth centuries AD. You can still see the impressive Roman city gate, bridge, amphitheatre, bath-houses and the imperial audience hall. Constantine I had his court here before becoming sole ruler of the empire.

Germany was a major wine-producing region. Rhineland and Moselle wines were transported by barges along the rivers. German glass was also famous and is found throughout the western empire, along with German pottery.

The Porta Nigra ('black gate') at Trier.

A Roman glass flask found at Cologne.

The River Danube:
Rome's Balkan Frontier

The river Danube was in flood because of the melting snows, but the emperor Constantius crossed it at the most suitable point on a bridge of boats and set about ravaging the lands of the barbarians.

(Ammianus Marcellinus, writing about an event in AD 358)

Detail of Trajan's Column in Rome, showing the Roman army in Dacia.

The Danube flows eastwards from Switzerland and Germany through Austria, Hungary, Serbia, Bulgaria and Romania. Like the Rhine, it was a major frontier of the empire. However, in AD 106, the emperor Trajan crossed the Danube into Dacia (modern Romania) and conquered the Dacians, taking many slaves. He created a new province and gained control of the local gold mines. Trajan's column in Rome shows his army in Dacia, fighting and building fortifications.

Gold coin with Trajan riding down a Dacian enemy.

Trajan's army also built a famous bridge across the Danube, designed by the architect Apollodorus. It was almost a mile long and stood on ten stone piers 46 m (150 ft) tall. The emperor Aurelian destroyed the bridge in AD 271 when the Romans withdrew from Dacia and the Danube, along its entire length, once again became the frontier. Forts such as Carnuntum (in Austria), Aquincum (modern Budapest in Hungary), Sirmium and Viminiacum (in Serbia),

Brass coin of Trajan showing bridge over the River Danube.

The Roman town of Durostorum on the south bank of the Danube.

Nicopolis ad Istrum.

Nicopolis ad Istrum (in Bulgaria) and Noviodunum (in Romania) were the bases for garrisons and ships for river patrols. These patrols did destroy some invading barbarians, but the pressure became so great at times that the Romans allowed peoples to enter the empire. In AD 376 the emperor Valens permitted a large force of Goths across the Danube. However, events got out of hand. The Goths defeated a large Roman army and killed Valens at the battle of Hadrianople in AD 378. This was one of the biggest defeats the Romans

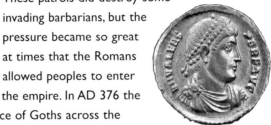

Gold coin of Valens (AD 364-78), who was killed by the Goths.

suffered. The Danube frontier did survive, although much of the western part was lost in the fifth century. The eastern half continued to exist into the later Byzantine period when the emperor Justinian the Great (AD 527–65) fortified many of the military bases.

Split, the Palace of an Emperor

In AD 284, the Roman empire was close to collapsing. However, it was saved by the emperor Diocletian who was born near Salona in Illyria (modern Croatia). He created a 'college' of four emperors to rule the entire empire. In 305, he retired to his homeland and built a fortified palace at Split on the Adriatic coast. He was one of very few emperors who survived into a peaceful retirement. It is said that his favourite hobby was growing cabbages! He was buried in a mausoleum (huge tomb) which still survives, along with other impressive remains.

The Mausoleum of Diocletian at Split, later converted into a church

A bronze coin of Diocletian which marks his retirement in AD 305.

19

Turkey: Mother of Cities and Religions

Great is Diana of the Ephesians!   (Acts of the Apostles)

Modern Turkey is a vast and diverse country that contained several different Roman provinces. The Romans called western Turkey 'Asia'. Asia was left to Rome in the will of King Attalus of Pergamum in 133 BC, to save his people from an inevitable Roman invasion. Rome gained much more territory in Turkey after Pompey the Great defeated King Mithridates in 63 BC.

Copper coin showing Pompey the Great.

Before Rome arrived, Asia was already called 'The Mother of Cities'. Her cities were to become even grander in the Roman period as rich people, and even emperors such as Hadrian, funded major building programmes. Asia was also a source of marble for building throughout the empire. Visitors can still see wonderful Roman remains at Pergamum, Priene, Miletus and Aphrodisias.

Ephesus was the provincial capital of Asia. From the site of the ancient harbour, you can still walk past gymnasiums and baths up to a massive theatre that seats 5,000 spectators. Here St. Paul attempted to convert the people of Ephesus to

Silver coin of Hadrian showing Diana of the Ephesians.

The stadium for races at Aphrodisias.

Christianity, but was opposed by the silversmiths who made souvenir statuettes of their goddess Artemis (known to the Romans as Diana). Her temple, one of the Seven Wonders of the Ancient World, stood to the north of the city.

The Actors of Dionysus perform in the theatre at Ephesus.

Modern visitors can still see the ornately decorated Library of Celsus, donated by a rich private citizen. Curretes Street leads you up a steep slope past fountains, temples, private houses and brothels, before you arrive at the main market place where there are further temples and the council chamber.

The Library of Celsus at Ephesus.

Walking through Ephesus today, full of modern tourists, gives you a feeling for the large, bustling cities that grew across the entire Roman empire.

The Temple of Hadrian at Ephesus.

New religions for Rome

Coin showing Cybele, the Great Mother, holding a drum and seated between two lions.

Cybele, the Great Mother, was an Asian fertility goddess who also cured and protected her followers. Her first temple in Rome was built around 200 BC, but it took many years for Rome to accept fully this new eastern religion. Mithras, another eastern god, came from Persia, but his religion was developed into Roman form in Turkey. Mithras was associated with the sun-god and was a warrior who stood for justice. His worshippers were all men. They had to progress through different grades, such as 'Soldier', 'Raven' and 'Runner of the Sun'. Worshippers ate ritual feasts, had to obey a strict moral code, and were promised life after death. Mithraism was very popular throughout the empire between AD 100 and 300, especially with soldiers and merchants. You can still visit temples of Mithras in London, and on Hadrian's Wall.

Statue of Mithras sacrificing the bull, from Rome.

Syria and Arabia: Luxuries for Rome

At the lowest reckoning, India, China and the Arabian peninsula take from our Empire 100 million sesterces every year: this is the amount our luxuries and our ladies cost us.

(Pliny the Elder, *Natural History*)

Rome gained control of the eastern Mediterranean gradually. Pompey the Great created the province of Syria in 63 BC, but he allowed independent kingdoms to remain in the region. Only after Trajan created the province of Arabia out of the kingdom of the Nabataeans in AD 106, did Rome have full control of the region.

The 'Treasury' in the Nabataean capital of Petra.

Coin of Trajan, celebrating his conquest of Mesopotamia in AD 115, showing the emperor standing triumphant over figures representing Armenia, the River Euphrates and the River Tigris.

Further east, the Romans faced the formidable Parthians with their mounted archers. The Parthians destroyed Crassus's army at Carrhae in 53 BC. Later, Rome did get the upper hand and briefly occupied Mesopotamia (modern Iraq) under the emperor Trajan (AD 98–117).

Soon after the fall of Parthia, in around 226, a new threat emerged, the Sasanians from modern Iran. They defeated several Roman emperors and their king, Shapur, even captured the emperor Valerian in AD 260 and used him as a footstool before having him stuffed after he died!

Latin was never the main language in the east. Instead, Greek was spoken by the richer classes and Syriac and Aramaic by the poorer people.

A rock carving in Iran showing the Sasanian king Shapur victorious over the Roman emperors Philip and Valerian.

From the eastern provinces came purple dye from Tyre, linen from Laodicea, woollen goods and plums from Damascus, glass from Sidon and dates from Jericho. Major luxuries were imported from further east. Through cities like Petra, Damascus and Palmyra came silk from China, pepper, cotton, garnets and emeralds from India, and incense and myrrh from Arabia. In return, as Pliny has told us, Rome paid out enormous sums of gold and silver.

Silver pepper pot in the form of an empress found at Hoxne in England.

Incense burner made by the Sabaeans of Arabia, showing a camel.

Hair ornament made of gold, pearls and emeralds found in Tunisia.

Palmyra – caravan city of the east

Palmyra was to become one of the richest cities in the empire. It stood at the western end of the Silk Route that went all the way to China. Large caravans of camels laden with goods passed through the city, making it very powerful. This is shown by the magnificent buildings and ornate sculptures. Queen Zenobia of Palmyra even briefly ruled Roman territory in the east in the AD 270s.

Two modern 'Legio II Augusta' re-enactors dressed as Palmyrene women. They are standing in front of the tombstone of a British woman, who is also dressed as a Palmyrene.

Left: Stone bust of a Palmyrene woman, called Tamma, wearing silk clothes and rich jewellery. The stone is inscribed in Aramaic.

Monumental arch in the city of Palmyra in the Syrian Desert.

Judaea – Revolts against Empire

Hadrian, 'may his bones rot'   (Jewish rabbinical literature)

In the time of Augustus, Judaea was ruled by King Herod the Great (40–4 BC). Herod was an ally of Rome and was one of the greatest builders of the ancient world, constructing numerous palaces and the great harbour at Caesarea. In AD 6, soon after Herod's death, the Romans took over Judaea. The Romans were often ineffective and tactless, and this resulted

An aerial view of Caesarea Maritima in Israel showing Herod the Great's harbour.

in the outbreak of the first Jewish Revolt in AD 66. It took the Romans, under the future emperor Titus, four years to capture Jerusalem.

Titus and his father, the emperor Vespasian, held a spectacular triumph in Rome, parading the spoils from the Jewish Temple in Jerusalem. The Jewish people were also now ordered to pay their religious taxes to the Roman god Jupiter.

The Roman siege-ramp which was used to storm Masada in AD 73, bringing a final end to Jewish resistance in the first Jewish Revolt.

A coin of the emperor Vespasian with the inscription JUDAEA CAPTA (Judaea captured) celebrating the crushing of the first Jewish Revolt.

Bust of Titus, who put down the first Jewish Revolt.

A second Jewish Revolt occurred in Judaea in AD 132–5, during the reign of Hadrian. Led by Simon Bar Cochba, the Jews objected to the building of a pagan city over Jewish Jerusalem and to Hadrian banning circumcision. The emperor crushed the revolt and hundreds of thousands of Jews lost their lives. Many fled to caves in the deserts. Afterwards, Hadrian renamed the province Syria Palestina and named Jerusalem 'Colonia Aelia Capitolina' after his own family name, Aelius. This is why Hadrian was so hated by Jewish writers.

Silver shekel of the Second Jewish Revolt with an image of the Temple that had been destroyed in the First Jewish Revolt.

Loot from the Temple in Jerusalem, including the Menorah, from a carving on the Arch of Titus in Rome.

The Arrival of Christianity and Islam

Jesus Christ preached in Judaea in the AD 20s and early 30s. Centuries later, Constantine the Great (306–337) made Christianity the official religion of the Roman empire. Many pilgrims, such as Constantine's mother St. Helena, began to visit the Holy Land, and the Church of the Holy Sepulchre in Jerusalem was built where it was believed that Jesus was crucified and buried. Jerusalem finally became the centre for a third great international religion when the Moslem Arabs captured the city in AD 636, building the Dome of the Rock about fifty years later.

A coin of the empress Helena, mother of Constantine the Great (AD 306–37).

Head of Christ on the Hinton St. Mary mosaic, c.AD 355, England.

Jerusalem showing the Dome of the Rock built on top of the Jewish Temple Mount.

Egypt: The Emperor's Province

Caesar came rejoicing to the land of the Nile, heavy laden with the cargo of law and order and prosperity's abundant riches

(Inscription on a statue of Apollo at Alexandria)

Egypt was the last kingdom of Alexander the Great's empire to fall to Rome. Queen Cleopatra of Egypt had close relationships with two of Rome's most powerful men, Julius Caesar and Mark Antony. Antony and Cleopatra made a bid to control the Roman empire, but Octavian (later called Augustus) defeated them at the battle of Actium in 31 BC.

Coin showing Cleopatra and Mark Antony.

Bronze head of Augustus, found at Meroe.

Augustus quickly took control of Egypt. He made it his own personal province. The head of one of his statues was looted by invading Kushite soldiers around 20 BC and was buried at Meroe, hundreds of miles further south in modern Sudan.

Augustus and other emperors exported ancient Egyptian obelisks which had adorned the temples of the pharaohs. Several of these were erected in Rome and Constantinople.

Roman emperors exploited Egypt for grain to feed the people of Rome. Roman fields can still be seen in Egypt. Egyptian papyrus beds also provided the material for paper that was used throughout the Mediterranean.

An Egyptian obelisk erected in Rome.

We can see some of the people of Roman Egypt, who were involved in all of these trading activities, from mummy portraits from the Roman period found at Fayum in Egypt.

The worship of the Egyptian goddess Isis became popular throughout the empire, even reaching Britain. She brought fertility, good fortune and life after death to her followers. Her consort, Serapis, who is shown with a corn measure on his head, was also worshipped for his powers of fertility and healing.

Isis was to become associated with the Virgin Mary, the mother of Jesus Christ, probably making Christianity more appealing to worshippers of Isis. The Coptic Christian church was founded in Egypt in the late Roman period and still exists today.

Mummy portrait of a Roman woman.

Bronze statuette of Isis found near Pompeii.

Temple of Isis at Pompeii, destroyed in AD 79.

A bust of Serapis set against the sun (Helios), with a corn measure on his head.

Coptic Christian textile showing a bird and a cross.

Stone for empire

Stone was quarried at Aswan, in the south of Egypt, and in mountains in the Eastern Desert. Stone columns up to 60 tonnes in weight were quarried and pulled by hundreds of mules across the desert to the river Nile, where they were loaded onto boats.

The Pantheon in Rome, with columns made of stone from Egypt's Eastern Desert.

Britain: Outpost of Empire

When I took over the empire chaos reigned everywhere;
I am leaving it at peace, even Britain.

(Septimius Severus, AD 193–211)

Britain held a special place in the minds of the emperors and people of Rome. The province lay across the Ocean and so the invasion of Britain by Claudius in AD 43 also required the 'conquest' of the sea. Roman writers described the Britons as being particularly backward and dangerous – therefore Claudius' victory over the Britons gave him much glory.

Bronze head of Claudius thrown into a river, possibly by the Boudican rebels in AD 60/1.

Claudius succeeded where the great Julius Caesar had failed with his expeditions to Britain in 55 and 54 BC. Other emperors such as Antoninus Pius (who built the Antonine Wall in Scotland around AD 143) and Septimius Severus (who died at York in AD 211) also celebrated victories in Britain.

Coin of Septimius Severus celebrating his victories in Britain, AD 208–11.

The Roman conquest of Britain was gradual and Scotland was never fully conquered. Queen Boudica of the Iceni tribe in Britain led disgruntled Britons in revolt against the Romans. She sacked the towns of Colchester, London and St Albans in AD 60–61, before she was finally defeated. The Romans then consolidated the province with a network of forts, roads and frontier-works such as Hadrian's Wall. Britain had a garrison of about 50,000 Roman soldiers, the largest in any province in the empire.

Cawfields Milecastle on Hadrian's Wall.

The Roman road on Wheeldale Moor, Yorkshire.

A 'curse tablet' which records Mintla Rufus's curse on the person who has stolen material for making a cloak.

Many Roman towns were built in Britain. London was founded soon after the Roman conquest, which began in AD 43. Today, any place which ends with words such as 'chester', 'castor' or 'caistor' was once a Roman fort or town. Latin became the main language of administration, as shown by the Vindolanda writing tablets and by curse tablets found at Bath and Uley.

Many metals were mined in Britain: gold, silver, copper, lead, zinc, tin and iron. You can still visit the Roman gold mine at Dolaucothi in south Wales. We learn from a Roman price list that British woollen overcoats and British beer were exported elsewhere in the empire.

A representation of Winter dressed in a hooded overcoat and carrying a hare, on a mosaic from Chedworth villa.

Wealth of Roman Britain

From about AD 270, Britain became one of the wealthiest western provinces. Roman farms began to increase in size, possibly because farmers became richer as Britain exported more food to the Roman army on the Rhine frontier. We know that in the AD 360s, 600 grain barges were sailing the North Sea to Germany. This wealth is shown by several rich hoards of silver found in Britain, including the Mildenhall treasure that was buried around the time Rome lost Britain, about AD 410.

The Great Dish from the Mildenhall Treasure.

End of Empire

As long as the Colosseum stands, so shall Rome,
When the Colosseum falls, so shall Rome,
When Rome falls, so shall the world.

(The Venerable Bede, *A History of the English Church and People*, 8th century AD)

From the 260s onwards, Roman emperors fought almost continual wars with their enemies on the Rhine, Danube and eastern frontiers. Also, there were some vicious civil wars, such as when Constantine fought his way to supreme leadership of the empire in AD 324. The city of Rome became increasingly remote and other cities more important, notably Trier in Germany, Milan and Ravenna in northern Italy, Antioch in Syria and especially Constantinople in Turkey.

Medallion of Constantine the Great, AD 306–337, the first Christian emperor and founder of Constantinople.

Constantine built Constantinople (modern Istanbul) between 324 and 330 on the site of the city of Byzantium on the Bosphorus. After 395, it became the capital of the Eastern Roman empire (later called the Byzantine empire). The Western empire was ruled from Rome and Ravenna.

The church and then mosque of Hagia Sophia on the skyline of Istanbul.

Between 395 and 476, the Western empire collapsed under the onslaught of barbarian invasions. The Visigoths led by Alaric sacked Rome in AD 410, before creating a new kingdom in Spain. The Vandals took North Africa in AD 439 when they captured Carthage, removing in one blow Rome's grain supply and largest tax income. Finally, the Franks began to carve out a new kingdom in Gaul and Germany.

Mosaic from North Africa with a Vandal horseman.

A few years after the last Western Roman emperor, Romulus Augustulus, was deposed in AD 476, Theodoric the Great of the Ostrogoths founded a new kingdom in Italy. However, he did preserve the Senate and many Roman laws.

The Eastern, or Byzantine, empire managed better. The strengthened walls of Constantinople were able to resist all barbarians, including the Huns, and the Byzantine empire still controlled most of the Balkans, the eastern Danube frontier, Turkey, Syria, Palestine and Egypt. Justinian the Great (527–565) was even able to re-conquer Africa, Italy and parts of Spain.

Mausoleum of Theodoric the Ostrogoth in Ravenna.

Coin of an Ostrogothic king, 534-6.

Coin of Justinian the Great showing the emperor holding a cross on a globe.

In AD 630, after almost thirty years of bloody wars, the Byzantine empire finally defeated its old enemy the Sasanians of Persia. The two exhausted empires were then easy prey to Islamic armies from the Arabian Peninsula. By around 650, Byzantium had lost Palestine, Syria and Egypt and the Sasanian empire had collapsed. By 711, Moslem armies had taken Spain. These invasions really brought an end to the Roman empire, leaving only a small Byzantine empire around Constantinople. Constantinople, however, did remain the capital of the Byzantine empire until it was taken by the Ottoman Turks in 1453.

Walls of Constantinople, built in the early fifth century AD.

Medal of Mehmet the Conqueror who finally captured Constantinople in 1453 and brought an end to the last vestiges of the Roman empire.

Further Reading

Richard Abdy, *Pocket Dictionary of the Roman Army*,
    British Museum Press 2008
Mike Corbishley, *The British Museum Illustrated Encyclopaedia
    of Ancient Rome*, British Museum Press 2003
Paul Roberts, *Pocket Dictionary Roman Emperors*,
    British Museum Press 2006
Katharine Wiltshire, *Pocket Timeline of Ancient Rome*,
    British Museum Press 2005
Richard Woff, *Pocket Dictionary Greek and Roman Gods and Goddesses*,
    British Museum Press 2003

For older readers:

Jonathan Boardman, *Rome: A Cultural History*,
    Interlink Publishing 2008
A.K. Bowman, *Life and Letters on the Roman Frontier*,
    British Museum Press, new edition 2003
Lucilla Burn, *Greek and Roman Art*, British Museum Press, 1991
T. Cornell and J. Matthews, *Atlas of the Roman World*,
    Facts on File 1982
Dana Facaros and Michael Pauls,
    Cadogan Guide to Rome and Central Italy,
    Interlink Publishing 2009
Valerio Litner, *A Traveller's History of Italy*,
    Interlink Publishing 2008
T.W. Potter and C. Johns, *Roman Britain*,
    British Museum Press 2002

You can find additional information by visiting the Interlink website:
www.interlinkbooks.com